The A B C of Puppy Training

The Basic Guides and Easy Steps for Beginners Who Love Dogs and Puppies

ISBN: 9798656713528

Table of Contents

Chapter One

Choosing the Right Puppy - The Different Breeds of Puppies.

A young dog is a puppy. Many puppies weigh between 1-1.5 kilograms, and some weigh between 7-11 kilograms. After birth, all healthy puppets proliferate. A puppy's coat colour changes as the Puppy grows, as is typically seen in races like the Yorkshire Terrier. The puppies are born from an average of 63 days of gestation. They are born in an amnion, and the amnion is bitten off and eaten by the mother dog. Puppies almost instantly begin to nurse. When the litter of a puppy exceeds six, mainly if one or more of them are apparent runts, it is essential as a human to intervene in the runts to ensure that they receive adequate nutrition and mother care. When they reach an age of one month, puppies gradually wean and start to eat solid food. The mother may regurgitate partly digested food for the puppies or encourage them to eat solid food. At this point, the mother typically refuses to care, although she may sometimes encourage them to take care of themselves. First of all, puppies sleep most of their time and eat the rest.

Puppies are born with an entirely usable scent. You can't open your eyes. For the first two weeks, the senses of a puppy are fast rising. At this level, the nose is the primary sensory organ used by puppies to locate and find their mothers' teats if separated within a short distance—female open their eyes about 9 to 11 days after birth. At first, the retinas are poorly formed, and you have a terrible vision. Both adult dogs and puppies are not visible.

Furthermore, the ears of the puppies remain sealed up to approximately 13 to 17 days after their birth, after which they respond to sounds more actively. Dogs usually start to growl and bite and wand their tails and bark about two and four weeks old. During the first three months, Puppies increase, especially after their eyes and ears are open and not fully mother dependent anymore. They develop their coordination and energy, ignite their fellows and start exploring the world from the nest.

You eventually agreed to introduce a young, furry member to your family after much debate. You have checked dog breeds to find a respectable breeder with a litter of new pups and found one to match your way of life. You now have to choose the right Puppy in the litter, the last step to get the Puppy. No ideal "puppy check" is required to find the litter pick. Concentrate instead on finding the dog you and your family need. While every Puppy is amazingly sweet, not everyone suits you well. You will find a dog that will make a significant addition to the family with proper research and planning. To be based on puppy love, at first, sight is much too remarkable to make the decision. The incredible variety of races, training needs and temperaments makes your homework imperative. Each Puppy is ultimately adult, so it's the best way to make sure that your decision doesn't end in disappointment to choose a dog that suits your lifestyle. You'll have a clearer understanding of the puppies are likely to grow up to be and which might make right jogger partners after taking the time to study and compare dog races.

Different Breeds of Puppies

Companion Dogs: Every breed was developed for a cause that is no exception to the companion dogs. Their job is to keep your company, perhaps a dog's most important job. They are majorly friendly. Many of them are smallish versions of working dogs, and some were only built as adorable lap dogs — but they're all dogs without exception. Examples are the American Eskimo, Bichon Frise, Boston Terrier, Chihuahua, Coton de Tulear, Dalmatian, Havanese, Lhasa Apso, Papillon, Poodle, Pug and lots more.

Herding Dogs: The dogs were trained in this group to manage large cattle and sheep. They retain the skill still, although most of them never seen a Merino or Longhorn. They are robust, intelligent and severe advocates of family unity, and they love nothing better than seeing the entire family together. Examples are Appenzeller Sennenhunde, Australian Kelpie, Bohemian Shepherd, Sheepdogs, Briard, Cannan Dogs, Mountain Dogs etc.

Hound dogs: The oldest form of hunting dog is maybe the hounds. There are two types: the ones who hunt by sight or sighthound dogs and the ones who hunt by scent by smell. The sighthound dogs of this category are smart and swift, while the scent hounds are more like rugged and powerful off-road vehicles. Examples are The beagle, Bloodhound, Borzoi, Dachshund, Greyhound, English Foxhound etc.

https://www.pinterest.com/pin/796926096544227486/

Mixed Breed Dogs: Meet the real underdog that ends in a shelter far more than a mere purebred race. Adopting a mixed-race is honouring the little guy's uniqueness and origin. It also means that you are giving a home to a dog who needs a home. They are gotten from mating two different breeds together.

Sporting Dogs: They are always active and alert, in the dog world, sporting dogs are the hunters: the Pointers, Retrievers, Setters, and Spaniels. Most of them can multitask, but in general, Pointers are used to find and silently point game out; Retrievers bring out the downed game from either land or water; Setters find, point, and sometimes flush out of the hiding game; and Spaniels find and flush games. Examples are Barbet, Brittany, Spaniels, Vizsla, Weimaraner etc.

https://www.pinterest.com/pin/800937114964073342/

Terrier Dogs: Terriers are the canine world's rascals. Its name is derived from the Latin word terra (Terra), meaning ground, and refers to its love of searching for foxes, moles, badgers and rats. Terriers come in different sizes and forms, but they all share an energetic and feisty personality. Examples are Pitbull, Terrier, etc.

https://www.pinterest.com/pin/315322411413978483/

Working Dogs: The different dogs depicted in this community were born to carry out a wide variety of duties, from carts or slides to protecting people, property and livestock. They are usually robust, intelligent and fearful, and they can be funny or serious. They need a stable home and an intense, equal, quality training and care because of their size and strength. Examples are American Bulldogs, shepherd Dogs, Boerboel, Mountain Dogs, Boxer, Great Dane, etc.

Things to look out for when getting your Puppy.

Once determined which dog breeds the best match your home, you will have to pick a chip on which to select from a litter. I suggest you look at your nearest animal rescue shelter! There are some essential things to look for, whether you've picked a hybrid or a purebred dog:

Confidence and Activity Level

It is essential to monitor the behaviour of the pups before alerting them about their presence when you first visit the litter. You should look for a puppy who is not overly submissive or dominant with the other pups.

Sociability and Temperament

If you first connect with puppies, search for those who are coming close to you. These are indicators of well-rounded young pups who are beginning to live correctly. Some checks can be performed to check the sociability of a pup.

Taking each of these pups and measure their responsiveness. They should not struggle too much or nip and vocalize so that they can relax in your arms reasonably quickly. Manipulate their feet, legs, and mouths even to test that they are not too reactive. Another good check is to keep them down 30 seconds by holding them to the ground, initially, they may not like it, but they wouldn't muzzle or respond too much, and they would relax under your mild pressure. This takes some ability and confidence — for adults to do so. Make sure you don't pick the frighteningly shy dog. It's challenging to adjust this frightening element, so it's worth preventing if you have the potential to train a lousy dog to give him confidence successfully. The ideal Puppy will be with you and follow you and play with you at the start.

Health

Here are things to look out for to ensure that you are selecting a healthy pup:

The puppies should be well-rounded and should have healthy, shiny skin or coat. The puppies shouldn't be too skinny, neither should they be too fat; Examine the Puppy physically and ensure that it doesn't have an undershot jaw or overshot jaw; Its eyes, ears and genitalia should be free with no inflammation.

Take your two or three pups aside to check the vision and hearing separately. This can be done if you press, clap or drop something behind them to see if they react. You may also check their vision by placing a reward or a toy near them on the ground, to make sure they can see and locate it. All the papers to show the pup are of the highest standard should be used by a successful breeder. I will, however, also recommend a simple veterinarian test just to be 100 % positive of your last safety and health issues decision.

Upon assessing the entire litter, focus on a single dog, isolate the Puppy from the rest in the litter and look closer. Pay serious attention to these areas.

Eyes: No redness or drainage should be in the eyes. No loss of hair should occur around your eyes. The Puppy should not tingle, squint or rub at his eyes.

Ears: No odour or discharge may occur to the mouth. Good hair will cover the ear flaps. Scratching in the ear is an indicator of trouble.

Nose: It's OK that the nose has slightly clear discharge, but uncomfortable and discoloured drainage is not natural. The Puppy should be able to breathe from the nose quickly and noiselessly.

Head: There is a small low spot on the top of the head. This may suggest potential issues with "open fontanels" if the soft area is greater than one dime.

Mouth: The pup's gums are moist and purple (mucus membranes). The top and bottom teeth should align without a specific undercoating (for example, Bulldogs, Boston Terriers, Beijing) in the pup.

Body Wall: Look at the underbelly of the pup for a protrusion of an umbilical hernia around the naval. It may mean surgical correction if anything points out in this field.

Skin: During the screening, you looked at the coat. See the individual Puppy now more closely. No hair loss, pustules, redness, or flattening are supposed to occur.

Many people don't think about how necessary it is to get your dog at age 7-8 weeks. It is the start of the FORMATIVE PERIOD and is the period that your dog is most important to develop. This is the transition time for the wolf (and dog alike), and the pups are going to leave the den naturally and start joining the rest of the pack. You and your family are basically 'the pack,' and that is when you can make or break your pup during the formative period. When you skip this crucial formative phase, you risk getting an unsocialized dog that has behavioural issues such as an attack on people or other pets, hyperactivity, no warning or no comprehension of boundaries. During this time, socializing your Puppy with many different people of all ages, races, sexes and animals of all kinds (cats, chickens, stock if you live rurally etc.) is crucial. It is also time to teach your Puppy all the necessary skills you need for a lifetime.

Chapter Two

Materials Needed for Training your Puppy.

You are all ready to welcome a new puppy or dog into your home, including working together with him on his manners. Get your training supplies prepared before he goes home, so you are ready to begin your training on the first day. Here are my essential dog training tools and a couple of additional items in your arsenal you could want.

Clicker: A clicker may be used both in response to a hit and when this happens naturally to mark the desired behaviour. Clickers are available in various shapes and sizes, including handheld and wrist bands. Some leashes come even with integrated clickers. Clicker apps are also available for your smartphone and multi-dog clickers with different sounds per pooch.

Target stick: A target stick can help teach simple behaviours, such as leasing or complicated tricks such as spin or bow. Targets vary from an essential, extended, fixed to a beautiful item, like a bolt with an integrated clicker or a stick with a secure storage unit. A simple DIY target can also be a serving spoon or a wooden spoon – or you can save your equipment and teach your dog a touch and a hand target.

Treats: Rewards are exciting and encouraging for your dog. The care choice is different depending on the canine, but soft meat is generally a favourite for canines. Treats of the size of a pencil eraser or a blueberry should be tiny. Some therapies are pre-made for training, while others may be broken or measured before training.

Portable mat: Your dog should be put in a portable mat or bed, no matter where it is. Secure mobile and suitable for vacations, is a foldable, washable pad, a mat or blanket. Species with an adhesive surface tend to give improved stability on slippery surfaces.

Leashes: Exercise leashes typically range in length from four to six feet. Ideally, the leash is long enough to make your dog sleepy while he stays near you on walks (instead of continually being tight). A waist clip leash helps you during training sessions to keep your hands free—store leashes for your dog in simple positions like hooks by the entrance.

Collar and harness: A flat collar has the ID tag for your dog, which is vital if he is alone. A front-clasp harness is a safer option for most dogs though you can also clench leash on a flat chain as it will help avoid pulling and make mobility easier for your dog. A head stopper can be a helpful tool for hard-to-control dogs. (Note: corrective collars are not recommended during training.)

Longline: If the dog is prepared to practice long-distance stays and comes if called, a long line is a healthy and straightforward alternative to being without a leash. Long lines also provide explorations and additional space for activities such as scent detection during training breaks. Standard lines vary between 15 and 30 feet.

Barriers: Crates, pet gates, animal pens and playpen might be helpful for situations such as house training or chewing management if you need to hold your dog in a particular area. A barrier can also help to keep your pooch away from trouble areas such as the stairway or doorway.

Toys: Plays and toys are great rewards to be used in training for playful canines. It is attractive to your particular canine depends on the right types of toys. Keep your favourites on hand for a good job.

Treat bag: Training bags are a simple way of keeping treatments ready for your dog if desired behaviour occurs immediately. Stockings can be made of neoprene or other easily washed fabrics in size and design and attachment. Other bags have extra bags with zippers and velcro, for example, cleaning bags, keys and cellphones. A pinch can be used as a wearable holder of a fanny pack or jacket with extra pockets.

Food puzzles: Food puzzles have a physical and mental stimulation for your dog so that undesirable behaviours are avoided. You will even help your dog relax and relax while he is at his place or crate.

Chapter Three

House Training your Puppy and the Different Basic Training.

From the time you bring it home and begin house training. You should start to train your Puppy immediately. Puppies start learning from birth, and good breeders start socializing immediately. Some training will start once the Puppy can open his eyes and walk. Young puppies have a short period of training, but they can expect to start learning simple commands for obedience like "down," "down" and "stop" as soon as they are 7 to 8 weeks old. Traditionally, formal dog education was postponed until the age of 6 months. This young stage is a challenging time to get off the ground. The dog learns from all experience, and a delay in training means that the dog has missed the opportunity to learn how it will be. The dog starts to solidify adult behaviour patterns during the young stage and advances through times of fear. Comportements that have been learnt in puppies may need to be changed.

Furthermore, anything learned or improperly trained must be undone and retrained. Pups can learn a lot from their early years. When training begins at age 7-8 weeks, use methods which rely on positive strengthening and gentle instruction. Puppies have short care periods, so training should be brief but should take place daily. Pups can be taught how to "sit," down and stand to employ a method known as food-lure training. We use food treatments to make the dog sit, stand and stay in the right position to follow the nose.

How do I get started using food lure training?

Small snacks or a favourite toy can be used to inspire the dog to do most items. Provided that the prize is attractive enough, the Puppy can be encouraged to respond by showing the prize, ordering and moving the prize to obtain the reward. For instance, food held over the nose of the Puppy and moving backwards slowly should be replied "sit"; food drawn down into the ground should be replied "down," the food that is retrieved should be replied 'standing,' food held away should receive a "coming" response. Food held at the thigh as you walk should make the puppy 'heel' or 'follow.' The Puppy should learn the significance of each command soon by combining a command sentence or word with each action and paying the reward for each appropriate response.

Ideally, the command phrase should be said once while you use your food only to push your Puppy into positions. After the Puppy has done the task, add verbal praise and a loving pat, known as the secondary armour. You probably go a bit too fast if the Puppy does not immediately follow the first command. The Puppy will learn that several repeats are acceptable before he needs to keep the command repeated. If the Puppy doesn't follow, it can be helpful to keep a lease attached. Mind your Puppy doesn't know the meaning of the word early on in training. Thus you could teach your dog to sit with the word bananas as comfortably as you could with the word sitting. The key is to link the word, "sit," with the effect of putting the rear end on the floor.

In the beginning, you will let the Puppy see the food that comes into your hand so you can focus on it and guide it. You can begin hiding your food in your hand, as your Puppy begins complying more quickly, but give the instruction and replay the motion or sign she has learnt to follow. The Puppy will soon expect the treat whenever she does the job. Then sign and give the command, but when the task is done, only give the Puppy an affectionate pat and reward with praise. Next, you can start to change the rate, praise "good dog" and maybe patting each time but randomly, maybe every three or four times. In time, either the hand signal or the instruction should be responded. The words 'good dog' and affectionate pat have been strengthened over time. They acquire more meaning and become reinforcement in themselves, as they were paired with food in the past. You need a secondary refurbishment because when your pet needs to obey, you won't always have food with you.

Moreover, you will have a puppy that only does the job after a treat when you rely on food to make your Puppy come true. At the first training, a variety of family members start in designated sessions all day long. For these training sessions, all bonuses should be saved. But you should start asking your Puppy to do the tasks many times over time.

You don't have to practice in a specific session every day. Instead, combine these activities all day long. At least 15 minutes of exercise each day is a target to aim for. These can be brief sessions of 5 minutes spaced all day. Seek to ask your Puppy to do these things with all the family members. Remember to try to train your dog in every room of the house. You want your puppy "sitting," "lying down," and "staying" anywhere, not just at the training site. Practice anywhere in the future that you want your Puppy to behave and relax.

Using these exercises as you incorporate the Puppy into your life. Ask your Puppy, for instance, to sit down before you collect its food, sit down and sit down before you let her into or out the door. There are moments when your dog is more likely to comply with it. In this way, the dog is always exercised, during the day, and consistent rules and interaction patterns are developed and who controls the resources is taught. Before it gets its daily needs, teach your Puppy, it helps to prevent problems. Telling your dog to sit before opening the door prevents it from running out of the door of jumping up. Be imaginative. Be innovative. You will pay off later because when you have a well-trained adult dog, the time you spent raising your Puppy would be worth it. To have a well-trained dog, for the first year of your Puppy's life, you need to devote yourself to improving the training activities almost daily. The more the Puppy is trained and supervised, the less chance it has to be misconduct. Dogs are not conditioned; they will behave as dogs if left to choose their actions.

When should I start socializing my Puppy?

Socialization will start immediately you get your Puppy, sometimes at the age of 7 weeks. In the socialization period between the ages of 7 and 14 to 16 weeks, the puppies usually embrace new individuals, other species as well as new circumstances. It offers a chance for a countless presentation, which will deliver meaningful and life-long memories. At that time, pounds are keen, exploratory and uninhibited, and this excitement must be used. Please ensure that during this time you protect your Puppy and make every experience meaningful, fun and not afraid.

How to housetrain your Dog or Puppy

Your dog or Puppy needs to be raised with patience, commitment and consistency. Accidents are part of the process, but you can get the newest family member on the right track within a matter of weeks if you obey these simple guidelines.

Establish a routine

Pups do their best regularly, like children. The timetable tells you that sometimes you should eat, playing times and doing your business. In general, for every month of age, a puppy can regulate its bladder for 1 hour. And you should keep it for two hours if your Puppy is two months old. Should not go longer than this bathroom breaks or an accident is expected.

Bring your Puppy regularly outside – for at least 2 hours – and when you wake up, play, eat or drink immediately.

Pick a place outside the bathroom and carry your Puppy to that location (on a leash) when your Puppy is relieving itself, using a specific word or phrase before you go, to tell you what to do—taking them off only after they have been gone for a long walk or some playtime.

Each time they eliminate outdoors, you praise your Puppy. Praise or offer treats, just remember to do it right after you are finished, not after returning. This move is essential because the best way to teach your dog what they deserve is to be rewarded for going outdoors. Make sure that they've done before rewarding. Puppies are harder to confuse, and they will forget to finish when you compliment them too quickly before they are home.

Place a daily feeding schedule for your Puppy. What goes on a schedule into a puppy comes on a schedule out of a puppy. Dogs need to be fed three or four times a day, depending on their age. Feeding your Puppy at the same time, per day, makes it easier for each of you to get rid of your Puppy at regular times.

Take a bowl with your dog water dish for about two hours and a half before you sleep to reduce the chance with relief throughout the night. For almost seven hours, most puppies will sleep without a break in their bathroom. When your dog wakes you up in the evening, don't do a lot about it; if you don't think it's time to play and won't go back to sleep. Switch on as low as possible and don't talk or waste any time with your Puppy.

Supervise your Puppy

Ensure your Puppy doesn't get a chance to soil at home; watch them while they are inside. If you're not actively training or playing, attach your Puppy to a nearby piece of furniture with a six-foot leash. See the signs your Puppy needs to quit. Some signs are visible, like barking or scratching the door, squatting, restlessness, sniffing or circling. When you see these signs, catch the rope straight away and take it to your bathroom. Lob them and reward them with a treat if they remove them. Hold the dog in the yard on a leash. Your yard should be handled like every other space in your house during the building training phase only after they are reliably trained to give your Puppy freedom in the house and the courtyard.

When you can't supervise, confine

When you can't always see your dog, limit it to a small area that you don't want to eliminate. Space should only be wide enough to stand, lie down and rotate comfortably. You may also use a bathroom or laundry room with baby gates closed. Or maybe you'd like your Puppy to be in a crate. You will have to carry your dog directly to the toilet when you return if it has spent a few hours in custody.

Wait for a few casualties in the house with your Puppy — this is a standard part of home training. What will I do if this happens? Take the punch off your dog, make a shocking noise (watch out not to frighten them) or yell "In!" and take them directly to their toilet. Love your dog and have a treat when they're done there; don't punish them by having your pet out of the room. It's too late to administer a remedy if you find a soiled area. Clean it up. Wash it up. The only thing they can hate, or want to eradicate in your presence will be rubbing the nose of a puppy into it and taking it to the site and scolding it or any other punishment. Sanctions often harm more than good; thoroughly clean the soil area. Puppies are highly motivated in places that smell like urine or faeces to start soiling.

To reduce the number of accident, you need to use these control and confinement approaches. If you let your Puppy in your house often remove them, they'll get confused as to where they're supposed to go.

You may not be able to get a puppy bach home when you have to be away from home for more than four or five hours a day. You may want to think instead of an elderly dog who can wait until your return. If you already have a puppy and have to be away from home for a long time, you're going to have to:

Arrange someone to take them for breaks in the bathroom, for example, a caring neighbour or a professional parent.

Train them to eliminate indoors in a specific location. Nonetheless, be mindful that this will prolong the recovery cycle. If you teach your Puppy to eliminate in the newspaper, you will establish a lifetime surface preference, which encourages him to remove any journal lying around the living room even as an adult.

If you intend to paper train your dog, confine it to a zone with ample space to sleep, play space and a separate area to eliminate. Use either a newspaper (cover a multi-layered region of the journal) or a sod box for the specified eliminating region. To make a sod, growing it in a tiny, plastic pool in a container. Dog litter supplies can also be sold in a pet supply store.

If an accident has to be washed up outside the planned disposal area, then add soiled rags or towels in the accident to assist your Puppy in knowing that the scented area should be removed.

Chapter Four

Understanding the Dog Language - Knowing What your Puppy Wants and How to Make Friends with It.

What does your dog want to say to you? Dogs have a language that allows them to communicate with others around them their emotional condition and intentions. When dogs are using sounds and gestures, much of the information they send is through their linguistic body, particularly facial expressions and body positions. Understanding what your dog is doing will provide you with many useful details, for example when your dog is talking and afraid about what's happening, or when your dog is edgy and might be about to hit someone. The dog's face and the entire body must be looked at.

Relaxed Approachable

This dog is happy and fulfilled. Any activities in his immediate environment don't affect the dog as the dog is usually unbothered and approachable. Nevertheless, caution is essential when trying to approach a new dog and do not rush to greet a dog even though they appear comfortable. Signs of the dog being relaxed are: Tails are down and relaxed while the ears are up (not forward) with the mouth open slightly and the tongue exposed.

https://www.pinterest.com/pin/11329436550524824/

Alert- Checking Things Out

If the dog senses something or anything unseen, the signals show that the dog is now aware and alert when assessing the situation to find out whether there is a danger or whether any action should be taken. Signs of dogs being at alert is the ears are forward and may twitch while trying to catch the sound of something, and eyes are wide, mouth closed while the tail may move slightly from side to side.

https://www.pinterest.com/pin/668432769670157146/

Dominant and Aggressive

This is an animal that is powerful and effective. He demonstrates not only his social superiority but threatens to act violently if challenged. You should know your dog is dominant or submissive, and can also be more mindful of how other dogs can behave around you. The signs are the tails are raised and bristled, ears are forward, nose wrinkled as well as the forehead, and the teeth are visible while the dog makes a Groaning sound.

https://www.pinterest.com/pin/291256300877449482/

Fearful and Aggressive

This dog is afraid, but not compassionate, and will strike when pressed. A dog usually gives these signs if he encounters the person who challenges him directly. Scared dogs can be hard. The body of the dog is lowered with the hackles raised, and tail tucked with little or no movement of the tail, ears back and pupils dilated. The nose is wrinkled with the lips slightly curled.

Stressed and Distressed

This dog is socially or environmentally stressed. However, these signals are an overall "broadcast" of his mind and are not directly addressed to any other human. The tail of the dog is down, and the back is lowered with the ears back. There is a rapid panting with the corner of the mouth back while it is sweating through the pads.

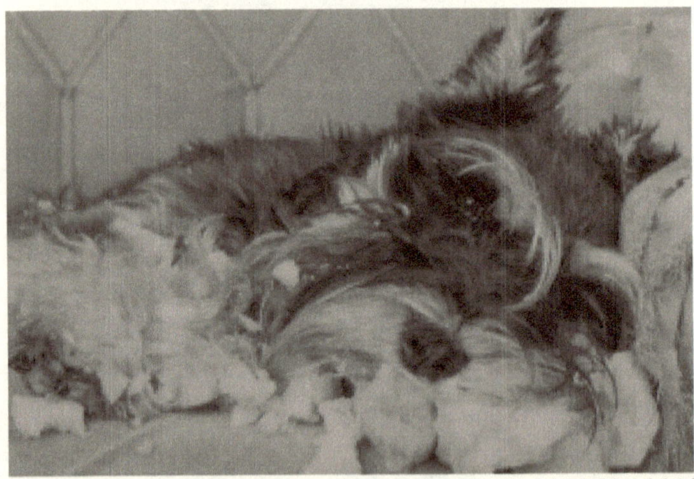

Fearful and Worried

This dog is a little frightened and gives signs of submission. Such signals are meant to calm people of higher social status or that the dog considers being potentially dangerous to avoid more problems and conflicts. If your dog always has these symptoms, you may not be comfortable and may have to try some extra tips to relax his anxious dog.

Playfulness

We have a fundamental invitation to play here. It may be accompanied by an aroused barking or playful attack. A collection of signals can be used to suggest that any previous raw action was not intended as a danger or challenge. The signs are the tail would be up while it waggles it, ears would be up, and pupils dilated, the mouth would be opened, and the tongue may be exposed.

https://www.pinterest.com/pin/307018899586821340/

Chapter Five

The Healthcare Essentials in Training your Puppy.

It's a beautiful time in your life, and I know you want to treat your animal the best you can. Puppies need to be looked after regularly like babies. In the first few months of life, this requires frequent visits to the vet.

Ideally, 6, 9, 12 and 15 weeks of age are to be vaccinated. Vaccinations are essential to prevent a range of fatal conditions: hepatitis, parvovirus, distemper, hepatitis and rabies. To be safe, puppies have to be vaccinated and at least annually after that. Moreover, several further vaccines may be suitable based on the situation of your pet.

At least two deworm treatments at the first two visits of your Puppy, followed by continuous treatment of heartworm and prevention of parasites. In puppies, worms and parasites are quite common, which can get infected in utero by mother milk. I recommend a faecal examination to determine if your Puppy has worms when you come to meet a veterinary doctor. Please take a stool sample if possible. To detect worms and other gastrointestinal parasites, a microscope will examine the sample. I also recommend that your young Puppy get a safe and effective deflated product two, three weeks separately, even without a faecal examination. The dewormer does not have any adverse effects and treats several common worms. Besides testing and treating any worms throughout your dog's entire life, preventive treatment of heartworms is also extremely necessary.

Spay or neuter your Puppy, depending on lifestyle and specie recommended for 4-6 months. Spaying or neutering can help to manage the problem of overpopulation and avoid other issues of health and behaviour.

Treat your dog to control fleas and ticks and also avoid them. Prevention and treatment of flea and ticks are essential to the health of your Puppy. The prescription drug is highly successful, but any treatment for the flea and tick should be performed cautiously to avoid undesirable and often severe reactions.

Create a balanced diet and practice routine. The basics of taking care of your young Puppy are nutrition and exercise. It depends on the individual circumstances how you feed and exercise your Puppy. Puppies usually need to eat in smaller amounts than adult dogs more frequently. Puppy food should be higher in fat and served for the first 12 to 8 months, depending on breed and size. Puppies need a lot of muscle development play and exercise.

Develop your Puppy's general care routine. Routine general canine treatment encourages the overall well-being of your Puppy. General treatment involves washing hair, bathing and toileting and burning teeth and to include long-lasting healthy toys.

Make your Puppy friendly and train it, making you both happy. Socialization and behavioural therapy are the secrets to a well-behaved dog.

Be conscious of risks and be prepared for emergencies. Safety and emergency preparedness helps you avoid risks and manage an emergency.

Chapter Six

Activities to Enjoy with your Puppy

Are you looking for easy ways to keep your dog busy and fun? It can be a challenge to keep your dog entertained. And it can be more tiring to find new ways for your dog to entertain than to get up and do it. Bored dogs get into trouble. Get into trouble. We are their primary entertainment source, and therefore if we don't give them things, they will do their activities-and this is when we get chewed up shoes and curtains. You will reduce the likelihood that your dog develops unpleasant habits such as repetitive barking or chewing by playing with your dog a few times a day. Here are some activities you can do with your dog.

Play a game of Find the Treats: Working nose games are among the best ways to get your dog out. You mentally drive them out and help them master some of the natural skills when you teach your dog to play simple nose games such as 'look for treats.' Take a few treats and then see your dog look for them around the room. Tell your dog to "find treats" and encourage your dog to pick them up, keeping in mind that every time you find one, you praise them. You can do it a bit more challenging when you have trusted your dog understands what "find treats." Let them stay in a different room as you hide the delights and hide them in places where they must sniff out like under teak.

Play the Shell Game: The shell game is an easy tool for dogs to solve. To play this game with your dog, let your dog hunt for a treat under one of three cups. The shell game gives the dog a lot of mental stimulation and allows them to focus on their problem-solving skills. The shell game helps them to solve problems.

Teach Your Dog How to Clean up its Toys: You should teach your dog to put their toys away if the toys are placed in a box. It might sound weird to teach your dog to clean up, but it's a lot of fun. Teaching your dog new skills increases their confidence and gives them more mental stimulation. When your dog knows "drop it" already, pick it up and bring it over the container until it is standing. Like crazy, compliment them, then rinse and repeat them. You have a dog that can clean up after himself eventually with consistency.

Make Use of a Stuffed Kong to Ensure Your Dog is Entertained: Stuffed Kongs, since they're so easy to prepare, are my choice to ease dogs' forbearance. When you want to ensure that your dog is busy for some time, try filling some of their favourite delicacies in Kong. You can ice a little bit of peanut butter, or broth in or just give your dog some therapies to operate on. There are several healthy treatments which are great for Kong stuffing if you've not known what to use. Using a stuffed Kong is an excellent way to keep your dog at work. Put in the freezer your stuffed Kong overnight and give it to your dog as you leave in the morning. For most dogs, a frozen Kong will take over 30 minutes — much longer if it is filled.

Play a Game of Tug of War: One of the best ways to play meaningful play with your dogs is to play a tug of war game. It is a great way to exercise your dog mentally and physically. You can play it indoors as it does not have to be a ton of space. And, contrary to what others suggest, tug-playing won't make the dog angry and won't make it dictator. Allowing your dog to win just makes your dog more fun and allows you to play more. Hogs playing tug with their owners were considered more loyal and trustworthy. The tug is an excellent way to play your dog when you obey a few simple rules, including "the game ends if your teeth touch my hind."

Teach it how to do chores: Dogs love a job, even if it's as simple as picking up your slippers. By telling them the names of other things that you would not care if you had considered them any more useful. You should tell your dog to pick something from the fridge if you wish to please your friends. Once your dog is trained to open the refrigerator, tie a towel around the handle to make it easier for them to open the fridge. And you can teach your dog to do chores every day if you want to feel like a superstar.

Play Interactive Games: I love interactive games like tug-in, finding treats, puzzle games and fetch for my dog during rainy days. Interactive games are a simple way to relax your dog and can help alleviate issues such as repetitive chewing or barking. Yet take it from me, use a lightweight ball to keep all things from breaking if you're going to play fetch inside. A tug game is a great way to increase your dogs' manner and a pulse control, and it's a fun thing for dogs. It's a pretty good experience as well. It's one of the most complicated games we're playing minute by minute.

Make Your Dog Work for His Food: I give an excellent comfortable life for my dogs — they have a warm bed, a great deal of attention and all their food free of charge. But my dogs have been brought up to work, and many of the dogs lack mental incentives. They are natural scavengers, so it's not mean or unusual to work for food – it's a healthy and mental stimulant for them. One of the easiest ways to challenge the mind of your dog is to get them to work for their food. You can do certain tricks to make your dog eat a food-dispensing toy before it gets its dinner.

Teach them their toy's names: Have you seen Border Collie's Chaser? She knows more than 1,000 words and can only select every toy by its name from 800. Dogs can't all be chaser overachievers, but we can teach our dogs their toys and play a lot of fun. Start playing with a particular toy and give it a name while you are playing. The dog will give this verbal name to the chosen toy after some practice and encouragement. After your dog knows that, you can test its skills by seeing whether they can pick it up among their other toys.

Teach your Puppy how to find its toys: If your dog knows any of their toys' names, then teach them the game "Go find it." In a pile or a tub, put your dog's toys and tell them to "play" their favourite pet. When your dog progresses in this game, you can make it more difficult by increasing the number of toys they have to screen. Keep it enjoyable for you by rewarding you well when you succeed with a treat or fast tug game. It is a perfect exercise for your dog.

Teach Your Puppy some New Trick: Does your dog know how to tweak and spring through your legs? You should always teach your dog a new trick and trust me when I say it is much easier than it sounds to teach your dog how to weave your legs. Your dog knows a lot of tricks already? Some of the essential things about trick preparation are that improvisation and pressure are still there. If your dog knows a lot of tricks, you can step it up and add new tricks to their experience.

Work on Some Clicker Training: A clicker is one of my favourite tips in dog training. It is a little box with a lever that makes a noise when you press it, and it signals the exact moment when your dog is exhibiting the action it needs. This is an easy way to make sure I let my dog know when she's doing the right thing, and I love using one. I would encourage you to pick up one next time you're at the animal shop if you don't have a clicker. It is so difficult to miss the chance to communicate with our dogs as quickly as they do the conduct you want when training a dog every second. You can determine when your dog has chosen precisely when you use a clicker.

Play a Game of Hide & Seek: The hide and seek game is one of the most popular games by far. Hide and seek May not all appear to us so complex or amusing, but many dogs get a real boot. You can ask a friend if your dog does not have proper command, to help by distracting your dog while you go and hide (or you can practice your "stay" before you get started).

Get Some Puzzle Toys For Your Dog: Take care of your dog by offering it a puzzle to solve. A lot of dog puzzles and games like the Kong Wobbler are available for dispensing. You can also make a lot of great DIY toys there. Simple muffin tin game I love, you're ready to play if you've got a muffin tin and some balls. Your local pet store would have the latest bully sticks and barebones if you want your dog to chew on. Only make sure that you are immune to smells while opting for odourless bully sticks.

Master the Basics of Obedience Training: Is your dog familiar with all the basic commands for obedience? Even trained dogs now and then need a refreshing course. Every dog should be able to, wait, stay, drop it, and get there. A few quick exercises (5-10 minutes) every day help your dog learn the basics and allow your dog to be mentally stimulated.

Play Fetch: Most of us have extra space indoors for a simple fetch game, but you probably should skip this game when living on the fifth floor with a St. Bernard. Popular options are when you play indoor fetching hallways, staircase and ample living spaces. With her Jolly-ball, my dog and I love to play football in the basement. Take care with big toys and things that are fragile or can be flipped, and not a good idea playing fetch in the kitchen. You could turn it into a simple catch game if you did not like the idea of playing house indoors.

Dog Massage: Learning how to massage a dog is both enriching for both the owner and the dog. Almost every dog can rest and relax with a good massage. And dog massages are excellent for elderly dogs or arthritis because they can help soothe sore and sore joints. A massage reduces anxiety, relieves stress, improves the flow and establishes a secure link between you and your dog.

Groom your dog regularly: Although your dog doesn't find a care session as exciting as a tug game, it has to be done occasionally. Our dogs must be cleaned up, bathed, washed their teeth and trimmed their nails as soon as they start getting longer. Some dogs endure better tolerance than others, and the easier it becomes to practise positive rewards. Do not be afraid of delivering plenty of care during treatment – you want to make sure your dog combines care habits with a positive experience.

Play a game called Tag: Playing Tag is a fun interactive dog game, but a partner is required. You will all sit or stand with a toy or some delicacies on one side of the room. Take turns and recompense the dog as he arrives. Make sure that every time your dog obeys, you keep giving your dog plenty of positive reinforcement. It's fun and straightforward to reinforce a trustworthy reminder.

Create Your Own Indoor Doggie Obstacle Course: Build in your home your obstacle course. Have your dog spring over towels, tweak his toys and then sleep on a blanket. Use your imagination and create several barriers to follow your dog. You then move into the toy fabric when your dog learns how to jump over the towel. Based on previous tricks, your dog will be mentally stimulated and focused.

Teach your Puppy to Chase Bubbles: This is my preferred activity when I am under the weather to keep my dog busy. It is so easy to please, enjoy and train my Puppy. I don't know why, but a couple of dogs' bubbles are fascinated. On the market, there is also a wide selection of animal bubble products. Neither do you go out and buy individual bubbles – children's bubbles are not harmful. Here is some evidence that babies, dogs and bubbles are the happiest things on the planet when you have a child at home.

Make a Doggie Play Date: Hope your dog has a few lovely friends? For some time, invite them to practice. It's so rewarding to see dogs playing, and at the end of the day you'll have a tired dog, it's pretty sure. You should even pick up some work as the dogs make their mania in your living room.

Chapter Seven

Conclusion

It gives you a marvellous pet when you train your dog at an early stage. Through working with them regularly, you can help the dog change negative behaviour. Consistency is the key to make the change your dog wants to see. Hold your rules and encourage nobody else to distract you from having a wonderful pet. If the dog is relaxed and follows its orders, you may feel less nervous. It is essential when they do this. You would be able to take them out and encourage them to be involved. Dogs are like children – you will continue to love and help them. Around the same time, you must understand that you must accept correction to be a positive family member.